HR APPROVED

WHAT YOU WANT TO SAY
VS
WHAT YOU SHOULD SAY

If you found yourself laughing at the absurdity of office life while reading, consider leaving a review!

What You Really Want to Say:

"I'm not your damn personal assistant, so figure it out yourself!"

What HR Wants You to Say:

"That falls outside my scope. Please take care of it on your end."

What You Really Want to Say:

"This is a complete clusterfuck."

What HR Wants You to Say:

"There seems to be a significant miscommunication here."

What You Really Want to Say:

"You seriously fucked this up."

What HR Wants You to Say:

"There's room for improvement here. Let's review the process together."

What You Really Want to Say:

"Shut up and let me speak!"

What HR Wants You to Say:

"If I could just finish my thought, I'd appreciate it."

What You Really Want to Say:

"I don't give a shit."

What HR Wants You to Say:

"This isn't my priority at the moment."

What You Really Want to Say:

"What the fuck were you thinking?"

What HR Wants You to Say:

"Can you walk me through your thought process on this?"

What You Really Want to Say:

"You're not being helpful at all."

What HR Wants You to Say:

"This approach isn't working for me."

What You Really Want to Say:

"How many times do I have to tell you?"

What HR Wants You to Say:

"This seems to require further explanation."

What You Really Want to Say:

"Do I have to do everything around here?"

What HR Wants You to Say:

"I'd appreciate it if you could take ownership of this task."

What You Really Want to Say:

"Stop being such a pain in the ass."

What HR Wants You to Say:

"Let's collaborate to make this process smoother."

What You Really Want to Say:

"That's the dumbest idea I've ever heard."

What HR Wants You to Say:

"I'm not sure that aligns with our goals, but let's explore other options."

What You Really Want to Say:

"I'm done with this shit."

What HR Wants You to Say:

"I'll need to step away for a moment to refocus."

What You Really Want to Say:

"You're pissing me off."

What HR Wants You to Say:

"I'm feeling frustrated. Let's take a moment to reset."

What You Really Want to Say:

"Are you fucking kidding me?"

What HR Wants You to Say:

"I'm surprised by this. Can you clarify?"

What You Really Want to Say:

"This is bullshit."

What HR Wants You to Say:

"I believe there's some confusion we need to clear up."

What You Really Want to Say:

"Get your shit together."

What HR Wants You to Say:

"I'd appreciate it if we could refocus and get back on track."

What You Really Want to Say:

"I can't believe I have to deal with your crap."

What HR Wants You to Say:

"I'd like to address the issues we're facing and work toward a solution."

What You Really Want to Say:

"Fuck this, I'm out."

What HR Wants You to Say:

"I'll need to take a break and revisit this later."

What You Really Want to Say:

"You're always screwing things up."

What HR Wants You to Say:

"We seem to be encountering recurring issues. Let's discuss a way to resolve them."

What You Really Want to Say:

"I'm not your fucking babysitter."

What HR Wants You to Say:

"I trust you to take responsibility for this task."

What You Really Want to Say:

"This is fucking ridiculous."

What HR Wants You to Say:

"This situation seems unreasonable. Can we discuss a better approach?"

What You Really Want to Say:

"You're an idiot."

What HR Wants You to Say:

"I think we're missing some key understanding here. Let's go over it again."

What You Really Want to Say:

"That's a load of crap."

What HR Wants You to Say:

"I believe there are some inaccuracies in that information."

What You Really Want to Say:

"Fuck off."

What HR Wants You to Say:

"I need some space to handle this."

What You Really Want to Say:

"That's not my fucking problem."

What HR Wants You to Say:

"This falls outside my responsibilities, but I can point you in the right direction."

What You Really Want to Say:

"What a shitshow."

What HR Wants You to Say:

"This project seems to have a lot of moving parts. Let's organize it more clearly."

What You Really Want to Say:

"Are you fucking serious right now?"

What HR Wants You to Say:

"I'm finding this situation surprising. Can you explain further?"

What You Really Want to Say:

"This is driving me crazy."

What HR Wants You to Say:

"I'm feeling overwhelmed. Let's break this down step by step."

What You Really Want to Say:

"You've got to be fucking kidding me."

What HR Wants You to Say:

"I wasn't expecting that. Can you elaborate?"

What You Really Want to Say:

"I'm not fucking dealing with this anymore."

What HR Wants You to Say:

"I'll need to hand this off or come back to it later."

What You Really Want to Say:

"This is a goddamn disaster."

What HR Wants You to Say:

"There are some significant challenges here. Let's figure out a way to fix them."

What You Really Want to Say:

"You're a pain in the ass."

What HR Wants You to Say:

"This situation is proving difficult. How can we make it easier?"

What You Really Want to Say:

"What kind of idiot does that?"

What HR Wants You to Say:

"That approach doesn't seem to work well. Let's try something else."

What You Really Want to Say:

"Who the hell do you think you are?"

What HR Wants You to Say:

"I'm not sure I understand your perspective. Can you clarify your position?"

What You Really Want to Say:

"I'm so fucking over this."

What HR Wants You to Say:

"I'm reaching my limit. Let's take a break and revisit this."

What You Really Want to Say:

"I couldn't care less."

What HR Wants You to Say:

"This isn't something I'm currently focused on."

What You Really Want to Say:

"Why the fuck do I have to fix everything?"

What HR Wants You to Say:

"I'd appreciate it if we could distribute the workload more evenly."

What You Really Want to Say:

"Get the hell out of my way."

What HR Wants You to Say:

"Could you step aside so I can take care of this?"

What You Really Want to Say:

"I'm not dealing with your shit right now."

What HR Wants You to Say:

"This isn't the right time to address this. Let's schedule it for later."

What You Really Want to Say:

"What the fuck is wrong with you?"

What HR Wants You to Say:

"I'm noticing some issues here. Can we talk through them?"

What You Really Want to Say:

"This place is a damn circus."

What HR Wants You to Say:

"There's a lot of disorganization. Let's work on improving efficiency."

What You Really Want to Say:

"I can't fucking believe this."

What HR Wants You to Say:

"I wasn't expecting this outcome. Can we review what happened?"

What You Really Want to Say:

"You're fucking useless."

What HR Wants You to Say:

"I think we can find a better way for you to contribute."

What You Really Want to Say:

"Who the fuck came up with this?"

What HR Wants You to Say:

"I'd like to understand who initiated this idea."

What You Really Want to Say:

"That's some real dumb shit."

What HR Wants You to Say:

"This idea doesn't seem well-thought-out. Let's reevaluate it."

What You Really Want to Say:

"I'm fucking done here."

What HR Wants You to Say:

"I'm going to take a step back for now and reassess."

What You Really Want to Say:

"Are you fucking brain dead?"

What HR Wants You to Say:

"I think there's been a misunderstanding. Let's clarify things."

What You Really Want to Say:

"This is the stupidest fucking thing I've ever seen."

What HR Wants You to Say:

"This doesn't seem to be the most efficient solution. Let's brainstorm other options."

What You Really Want to Say:

"You're such a dumbass."

What HR Wants You to Say:

"I think there's a gap in understanding here. Let's review the details."

What You Really Want to Say:

"Fuck this, I quit."

What HR Wants You to Say:

"I need to reassess my commitment to this project."

13470234R00030